Introduction

Job security isn't what it used to be. My Tax Preparation Business enabled me to become Financially Free in the first 4 month of the Tax Season. This book will do the same for you.

Chapter 1
Training To Become a Tax Business Owner

Running a Tax Business isn't only Tax Preparation. You must learn a number of other things before you open your doors for business, and get your first customer.

Chapter 2
The Checklist – This is the starting point to set up the

structure of your business. This Chapter will show you how to get your EIN, EFIN and your PTIN which are the prerequisites needed before you can open your Tax Preparation Business.

Chapter 3
You're Competitors - You really only have one major

competitor in the Tax Preparation Business. This Chapter will show you how to use your competitors to assist you in winning big. This chapter will also show you what other Tax Preparation Companies don't know about this competitors.

Chapter 4
Earned Income Credit is Great – Have you ever noticed that

most successful Tax Preparation Business are located in communities that have a high percentage of the population who qualify for the Earned Income Credit. This is not a coincidence. This Chapter will describe why Earned Income

Credit is considered the **Cash Cow** for the Tax Preparation Business

Chapter 5
Location, Location, Location - Show me a great location and I'll show you the money. There's a science in choosing the correct location to guarantee success. This Chapter will explain all of the attributes of a great Tax Preparation Business location.

Chapter 6
What Does the Perfect Tax Customer Looks like It's not what the customer literally looks like but their characteristics. This Chapter will give you the three main attributes of a perfect tax customer that will give you the highest profit in the least amount of time.

Chapter 7
Setting Up Your Office – You want your customers to be able to find you (Exterior) and once they find your location you want them to feel comfortable once they enter your establishment (Interior). This Chapter will explain the key area in setting up your Interior and Exterior of your Tax Business.

Chapter 8
Dealing With Customers Money – When Refund checks start to come in, your clients will want their money immediately. You as the Tax Preparation Company must be able to track the process of their Tax Return from beginning to end. This Chapter will give you key points to ensure your customer know their tax situation every step of the way.

Chapter 9

Choosing Your Phone Service – Just a business Phone number exclusively used for speaking during business hours is not enough. The correct phone service provides more than verbal communication. The correct phone service will provide you with extra tax preparation fees all year long.

Chapter 10
The Tax Season Time Sheet – Just like a High School student's class schedule informs you were a student will be every minute of the school day, the Tax Season schedule is similar. This Chapter will give you the blueprint for each day of the Tax Season and explain to you the exact days your customers will enter your business.

Chapter 11
Marketing Your Business – Just walking into your office and turning the open sign is not enough to drive customers to your business. This Chapter will explain the successful marketing techniques used by Tax Preparation Business to get customers running to their business.

Chapter 12
The Attributes Of The Effective Tax Preparer – Just because someone knows how to prepare taxes doesn't make them effective. The Tax Preparer that prepared taxes with a pencil and calculator is extinct. Hiring the correct Tax Preparers with essential skills, will ensure customer retention and money year after year. This Chapter will show you what that Tax Preparer looks like.

Chapter 13

Don't Be Afraid To Charge – Most Tax Preparation Business go out of business because of two things. If their Tax Preparation Fee are to low most will go out of business. If the Tax Preparation Business fees are too high the customers would either walk out or wouldn't return. This Chapter will explain how to price your service just righ

INTRODUCTION

Congratulations you have taken the first step to owning your own Tax Preparation Business. You've purchase the book and now you're ready to become Financially Free. I'm so pleased that you have chosen me to assist you on this epic journey. I won't let you down.

First, owning your own Tax Preparation Business will be challenging, but it can also lead to huge financial rewards. If owning your own Tax Preparation Business was easy, then everyone would have one and everyone would be Financially Free, but they're not.

I believe that in today's economy, only the people who are wise enough to own their own businesses will experience Financial Freedom and only when you are financially free, will you experience Job Security.

I know that everyone wants Job Security, and most people are of the belief that Job Security comes from someone giving them a job. However, I believe in the contrary.

In the past, Job Security use to be defined as that job you were able to depend on year after year. The job that would put your kids through college, pay off your 30 year mortgage, grant you that nice pension and gift you that Gold watch upon retirement. Those days are long gone.

Nowadays, Job Security is defined as being able to create your own business that will provide financial support for you, and your family. Just ask yourself, do you really have job security when you are employed by someone else. Suppose something happens to the company that you work for, like a company merger, or the business you work for decides to move overseas or even shut down. Can you really depend on that job to take care of you and your responsibilities? No!

At one time in my life, I too was depended on a job. However, I'm happy to say that I didn't give that particular job a chance to fire me before I figured it out. This book will show you how.

Something inside me knew that once I had a family, I would have to be able create a great income on my own merit. I was too afraid that once the time came for me to support my family, my employer would have the power to dictate my family's standard of living and I wasn't going to allow that to happen.

There are tremendous benefits in owning your own Tax Preparation Business, like being financially free, creating more time for you to spend with your family, leaving your successful business to your heirs and creating jobs for others. I describe these types of benefits as <u>Legacy Building Benefits</u>.

Answer this question for me. How many businesses do you know of that are recession proof, you may only have to work 4 months out of the year, you're off during the summer months and this business can be started with minimal expenses? That business is the Tax Preparation Business.

The main things that you'll need know or possess in order to be successful in a Tax Preparation Business will be the following:

- A Likeable Personality
- Be a Self-Starter
- A Computer
- A Great Location
- Printer, Copier, Scanner, Fax Machine Combo
- Internet Service
- Professional Tax Preparer Software
- A Preparer Taxpayer Identification Number (PTIN)
- An Electronic Filers Identification Number (EFIN)

If you happen to have that likeable personality and you're a self-starter that's great, because those are the only two things that I can't provide you with. However, I can assist you with everything else, so let's get started.

Chapter 1

TRAINING TO BECOME AN OWNER OF YOUR TAX BUSINESS

In order to have a successful tax preparation business, you must be a great owner. In order to be a great owner, you must be prepared for everything that can and will happen. Once tax season starts you won't have time to plan, you will only have time to execute.

Believe it or not Tax Season only last for approximately 100 days. It starts around January 15th and end approximately April 15th. Most new owners have the mistaken belief that they only have to work during the tax season to earn profits, however it's much different in real life.

To become a successful owner, your Tax Preparation Business will start way before the beginning of Tax Season.

I've found out through my own experience that the tax business owners that have everything planned in advance to the beginning of Tax Season and are ready to execute on the first day the IRS opens will usually be awarded the biggest profits.

Preparation can include but not limited to the following:
- Hiring and Training Tax Preparers
- Getting Marketing Materials Ready
- Installing Tax Preparation Software
- Setting up Payroll
- Purchasing Insurance
- Checking your E-file Status
- Knowing Your Competitors Locations
- Securing the Correct Location
- Knowing if your business is located in a high Earned Income Area

- Knowing how to deal with Low To Moderate Income Client
- Choosing the correct Phone Service
- Understanding the specific time frames for Tax Season
- Learning How to prepare taxes yourself

These are just a few things that a Tax Business must be prepared for, before they can open a profitable tax office.

Chapter 2

The Checklist

Complete the Following Steps to Open Your Business

Step 1. Obtaining the Employer Identification Number

Employer Identification Number (EIN) are issued for the sole purpose of tax administration and aren't intended for participation in any other activity. The EIN acts as the Social Security Number for your Business. It's a nine digit number with a format similar to the following (22-2222222)

Part 1. Determine Your Eligibility
- You may apply for an EIN online if your principle business is located in the United States or U.S. Territories
- The person applying online (www.IRS.gov) must have a valid taxpayer Identification number, SSN, ITIN, EIN.

Part 2. Understanding the Online Application
- You must complete this application in one session as you will not be able to save and return at a later time.
- Your session will expire after 15 minutes of inactivity, and you will need to start over if not completed.

Part 3. Submit Your Application
- After all validations are done, you will be given your EIN immediately.
- You can then download, save and print your EIN confirmation notice. A copy of your EIN will also be sent to you through the mail.

Step 2. Registering for your IRS e-Services account

E-Services is a suite of web based tools that allow tax professionals and payers to complete certain transactions online with the IRS. The tools include Registration Services, e-file Application, Transcript Delivery and TIN Matching.

The registration process involves collecting personal and taxpayer data for the sole purpose of authenticating your identity. The IRS will compare the information you provide with the information received from the Social Security Administration and with the tax return information you previously filed. The IRS will issue a registration confirmation code to you via the U.S. Postal Service, if the information you provide matches the IRS data. You must log back into the e-services web site within 28 days of the registration submission and enter this confirmation code to compete the registration process.

The IRS will ask you to provide the following information to become a registered user:

- Legal name (verified with IRS & SSA records)
- Social Security Number (verified with SSA records)
- Date of Birth (verified with SSA records)
- Telephone Number
- E-mail address
- Adjusted Gross Income (AGI) from either your current year or prior year filed tax returns (verified from IRS records)
- Username. Select your preferred username. Please read the rules for selecting your username
- Password and PIN. Select your password and PIN. Please read the helpful hints on selecting a secure, unique password and PIN
- Reminder question to recover a forgotten username
- Home mailing address (verified from IRS records). If you have moved since you last transacted with the IRS, please update your information when registering.

Please have this information ready before you start the process at www.IRS.gov.

Step 3. Applying to Become an Authorized IRS e-file Provider (EFIN)

Once the essential people are approved for e-services, your firm can begin the application to become an authorized e-file provider.

It's not a simple process, but a necessary step for tax professionals to understand in order to protect the integrity and security of the electronic filing system. All tax professionals have a stake in maintaining the highest standards for e-files providers.

The application is very comprehensive and it's designed so that you can save your data from a session, close out, and return to the application when convenient.

It can take about 45 days for the IRS to approve an e-file application. Please make sure you get your application filed early enough to start e-filing by the beginning of the tax season.

You will need the following important things to file:

- You will need your EIN for your company
- You will need to enter information about each Principal and Responsible official in your organization
- <u>You must choose your e-file options</u>. If you are a return preparer and want to e-file for clients, select electronic originator, or ERO.
- If the Principal or Responsible Official is someone who is certified or licensed, such as an attorney, CPA or enrolled agent, they must enter current professional status information
- All other individuals need to provide fingerprints to the IRS. You can get a fingerprint card by calling (866) 255-0654.

You must be fingerprinted by a trained professional like your local police station. The local police department will likely provide this service for a modest fee and there are commercial services that can provides the service for you. Upon completion, mail the signed and completed card to the IRS at:

Attn: EFU acceptance STOP 983
310 Lowell St
Andover, MA 05501-0001

Now your application is complete.

Step 4. Apply for a <u>Preparer Tax Identification Number</u>, PTIN from the IRS.

Anyone who prepares or assist in preparing federal tax returns for compensation must have a valid PTIN before they can prepare taxes.

<u>The PTIN Checklist</u>

Before you begin your PTIN renewal application, be sure you have the following information available:

- Personal information (name, mailing address)
- Business information (name, mailing address)
- Explanation for problems with your U.S. individual or business tax obligation (if any)
- Credit or Debit Card for the $50.00 PTIN user fee.
- If applicable, any U.S. - based professional certification information (CPA, attorney, enrolled agent, enrolled retirement plan agent, enrolled actuary, certified acceptance agent, or state license including certification number, jurisdiction of issuance, and expiration date.

Most PTIN correspondence are delivered through secure online messaging in your PTIN account. Use the most up-to-date email address when obtaining your PTIN to ensure that you receive our message.

Step 5. Complete the application requirement for <u>state electronic filing program(s).</u> Verify the application process for your state with the e-file Coordinator's office.

Step 6. Apply for any required state, city, local business license at least 30 days prior to opening. As part of this process, if required in your state, file a Fictitious, Assumed or Trade name for your business.

Step 7. Obtain Tax Reference materials from the state(s) for which you plan to prepare tax returns.

Step 8. Order <u>Publication 15 (Circular E)</u> – Employer's Tax Guide. Follow all federal payroll regulations as outlined.

Step 9. Research all states and local personnel/payroll regulations. Set up your payroll company (if applicable).

Step 10. <u>Order Business cards</u>. If you don't have an office location yet, use your home number or cell number as the point of contact. Make sure you order new business cards once you secure your office space and business phone numbers.

Step 11. Complete lease negotiations and arrange for any required leasehold improvements.

Step 12. Order your exterior signs.

Step 13. Order your Computers and network (If applicable).

Step 14. Arrange for your office phone number, phone system and internet installation.

Step 15. Arrange for utility connections.

Step 16. Open local business bank accounts

Step 17. Order office supplies, including client folders and client envelopes, for tax season by October 14th. Order 65% of your Tax Season supplies with your initial order.

Step 18. Acquire master copies of **IRS Employment Tax Forms** (I-9, W-4, state withholding, etc.)

Step 19. Acquire and display all required employment posters. They are available on the United States Department of Labor website or at Department of Labor offices.

Step 20. Install and configure Tax Software

Step 21. Purchase Business Insurance for your business

Chapter 3

HOW CLOSE SHOULD YOUR OFFICE BE TO YOUR COMPETITORS

Another major mistake that most new Tax Preparations businesses make when starting out is, trying to be as far away from their competitors as possible. When you think about it, that seems correct, but in most situations it's not.

Suppose you found a good location for your business but it was located in a community with a small population, a high income area, or a deteriorating community. Would you consider this be a great area to locate your business? Being close to some competitors may be wrong, but being close to a dominant competitor may be just right thing for a new Independent Tax Preparation Business.

I know you're aware of the largest Tax Preparation Company that has experienced the greatest success. That company is HR Block. The Block team is a big machine which has conducted so much research over time that they have mastered the art of being successful. The Block staff knows the populations of each community they serve, what people earn in each community, what language they speak and other necessary attributes so they can be successful. In other words, they have done all of the research for you.

There is a valid reason when you see a McDonalds Restaurant open in a community and soon after their opening other fast food restaurants follow suit. It may be a Burger King, a Taco Bell or any other popular fast food chain. Why does this occur? It occurs because the McDonalds machine has completed all of the necessary research and knows the exact area their restaurant need to be in order to become profitable. The same is true for Tax Preparation Businesses. Block has already done the research for you. By positioning yourself close to Block, you will more than likely receive the benefit from their extensive research. So don't think so hard and make sure you locate your tax business in the close vicinity of a good Block location.

Chapter 4

EARN INCOME TAX CREDIT IS GREAT

What Is the Earned Income Tax Credit (EITC)

The Earned Income Tax Credit, (EITC or EIC) is a Tax Credit designed to reduce the tax burden on working families. Its acts as a benefit for working people with low to moderate income. In order to qualify for EIC, you must meet certain requirements and file a US Tax Return. Even if you won't owe any federal taxes and you're not required to file a tax return, EIC reduces the amount of tax that's owed and may give you a tax refund. The tax refund comes in the form of a refundable credit which simply means that if the tax payer doesn't owe any money to the IRS, they will receive the remaining amount as a Tax Refund.

Requirements for EITC

One of the requirements to obtain EIC is that you must have earned income from a job in the year you are filing a US Tax Return. This income can be from employment for which you receive a Pay Check or from a business you own and operate under your Social Security Number called Self Employment.

Pay Check Employment

This is your normal job for which a company hires you, mandates a set time for you to work, and gives you a paycheck for which taxes are deducted from your paycheck.

Self Employed

Self-Employment is established by a person creating a job for themselves or working as an Independent Contractor.

People who create jobs for themselves may include occupations like Hair Stylist, Barbers, Lawn Care Service

Companies and Uber Drivers. These are jobs for which you work your own hours and get paid for your service.

An Independent Contractor is a person who usually has a specialty and contracts with a company or a person to do a specific job. They are not considered employees. These positions may include occupations like Real Estate Sales People and Free Lancers just to name a few.

You cannot earn EITC unless you actually work. For example: If you have money in the bank that earns interest, it doesn't mean that you qualify for earned Income. Although your money in the bank may have earned interest in the bank account it's the money in the account that earned income, not you.

Also most people believe they can receive EITC from Unemployment Benefits which is not true. Although you may have earned the Unemployment Benefits from working, Unemployment Benefits are considered insurance for not working, thus they won't qualify for EITC.

By following the outlined guideline ensures that the EITC is only given to people who need it, like Working Individuals, Working families, especially families with children.

Let me give you an example.

Jack is a single father that lives with his daughter Sally who is 10 years old. Jack works at McDonald's restaurant and makes $15,000 per year. Jack decides to have the normal Federal and State Income tax withheld from his check every pay period.

Jack is the perfect candidate for EITC because his wages are described as low to moderate and he's taking care of his daughter Sally who is a minor.

Jack's salary is mainly used for rent, groceries and day care. After Jack takes care of his basic needs, there is little or no money left for emergencies or for saving for his daughter's future. This is why EITC exist. EITC give a helping hand for low to moderate income individuals, especially low to moderate income families with children.

The only thing that Jacks needs to do is to file his US Taxes and make sure he claims the EITC on his tax forms.

Once Jack receives the EITC on his tax Refund, he will more than likely spend his refund to help support his family by purchasing, groceries, transportation, or either paying down debt. By doing this, Jack will also help the local economy by spending his tax refund on the things he needs.

What Are the Income Requirement for EITC (As of 2015)

Single or Head of Household Zero Children $14,820
Single or Head of Household One Child $39,131
Single or Head of Household Two Children $44,454
Single or Head of Household Three Children $47,747

Married Filing Joint - Zero Children $20,330
Married Filing Joint – One Children $44,651
Married Filing Joint – Two Children $49,974
Married Filing Joint - Three Children $53,267

The maximum amount of credit for Tax Year 2015 is:
- $6,242 with three or more qualifying children

- $5,548 with two qualifying children
- $3,359 with one qualifying child
- $503 with no qualifying children

The Tax Business Benefits of EITC

Like I said earlier EITC is the Cash Cow for the Tax Preparation Business. EITC is the main reason why I believe Tax Preparation Business do so well in areas where there is a high population of people who are likely to receive the EITC.

Location in Low to Moderate Economic Communities

There's no secret that in low to moderate economic communities you'll find a disproportionate amount of Tax Preparation Businesses. These are the communities where you'll find the people who work and have jobs with low to moderate wages. If there's a community with a large population of people that work for low to moderate wages, then they will more than likely qualify for EITC.

Provide A Much Needed Service To Help Get EITC.

The citizens in these Low to Moderate income communities are aware that even though they have low to moderate paying jobs, they may qualify for the EITC. To ensure that they receive the benefit, they enlist the help of a Tax Professional to file their tax returns and claim the EITC in the form of a Tax Refund

Charge a Higher Rate for Tax Preparation Fees

Tax Preparation companies understand that the people in the lower to moderate economic communities depend on EITC to help them every year. The people in the lower to moderate economic communities understand that their wages are low and they may also understand that may not have paid a significant amount of federal income taxes. However, they do understand that they still may qualify for EITC which may entitle them to thousands of extra dollars.

The Tax Preparation Business charge for the service and aid their client in receiving the EITC they deserve. Some fees range from $350 - $700 per tax return. So for instance, if a customer receives a tax refund for $8,000, the final check that they may receive if they went to a tax preparer to complete their taxes may be lowered to about $7,650 - $7,300 after the Tax Preparation Fee are withheld.

Chapter 5

LOCATION, LOCATION, LOCATION

One of the most important aspects in operating a successful tax business is the location. Choosing the correct location is essential for success.

It's much easier to have a successful tax preparation business in a good location than a bad location. When I refer to location, I'm referring to the VISIBILITY of your tax office. Of course there are several other factors that must be discussed in regards to your location, but the foundation to any successful Tax Preparation Office is Visibility.

What Does Visibility mean?

Visibility simply means how well your potential customers can see your tax office from the street level with very little effort.

The less effort your potential tax preparation customer uses to find your location, the higher your visibility which is equivalent to a better location. A great Tax Preparation office location, equals more customers and If you start your tax business in a good location, the less money you will have to allocate into advertising for new customers.

It's been studied that most tax customers decide which Tax Preparation Office they will patronize mainly by the Visibility of the Tax Preparation Office.

That means that most of your customers won't choose your office based upon loyalty with other brands, they will select your office by how easily it is to locate your Tax Preparation Office.

Some Factors That Go Into Evaluating a Location
(Each Section is rank 1st, 2nd and 3rd. 1st being the best choice and 3rd being the last choice.)

There are several factors that go into choosing the correct location that include the following:
- **Visibility**
    1st   Kiosk or Free standing building facing a busy Intersection.

 2nd Strip plaza facing busy road with a major Grocery/Retail store.
 3rd Smaller strip mall facing a major highway, or corner location on a busy urban street.

- Visibility within Mall or Strip Mall
 1st Directly in front of the center entrance, facing a busy road.
 2nd Next door to the mall's major anchor or grocery store.
 3rd In line with the mall anchor and parallel to the busy road, or on same hallway as anchor tenant.

- Signage
 1st Lighted, double faced sign on the main highway
 2nd Lighted single-faced box sign, large and visible from traffic.
 3rd Small, lighted single-faced box sign, less visible from traffic

- Commonly Known Address
 1st Major highway at a major intersection, or shopping mall a landmark
 2nd Major highway without a landmark
 3rd Secondary highway within sight of a landmark or major highway

- Accessibility for Customers
 1st Easy access from both direction with a stoplight in front of entrance
 2nd Easy access from both directions, without stop light
 3rd Access from one direction, ability to U-turn

without losing sight of the office.

- **Parking and Public Transportation**
    1st Mall with dedicated free parking in front of entrance
    2nd Available free parking within 100 yards
    3rd Metered parking within 100 yards

- **Vehicle Traffic per Day**
    1st Over 50,000
    2nd 35,000 to 49,000
    3rd 20.000 to 34,999

- **Location in Relation to Major Tax Preparation Locations**
    1st Located in the same mall or strip center
    2nd Less than ¼ mile away, within sight
    3rd More than ¼ mile away, out of sight

- **Size of Office**
    1st 600 square feet or less
    2nd 601 to 900 square feet
    3rd 901 to 1200 square feet

- **Lease Term**
    1st 4 month lease with option, or longer lease with a kick out clause ending April 30th.
    2nd 16 month lease ending on April 30th, kick out clause
    3rd 28 month lease ending April 30th, kick out clause

These are some of the factors that must be evaluated before selecting a great location.

What Economic Area Will Your Tax Preparation Business Be Located?

Another aspect that will determine how successful your Tax Preparation Business is choosing what economic area your business will reside in, "<u>Lower to Moderate Economic Class</u> or <u>Middle Class</u>."

Some beginning tax preparation business owners have no idea on how to choose which economic area to start a tax preparation business in. There are two levels of belief, but you as a small beginning tax preparation office must choose wisely and pick the best area for you to become successful immediately.

When I first started my quest to open a Tax Preparation Office, I wanted to choose a location in a Middle Class Community. I assumed that since the community was of Middle Class citizens, there would be enough economic support for my business. However, after careful analyses, I found out something different.

Middle Class Community v. Lower to Moderate Economic Community

Middle Class Community

Most Middle class communities are great because the citizens will more than likely have decent jobs and have income that taxable and tax returns will have to be filed on their behalf. However, Middle Class citizens are very particular on how they shop and who they patronize. The middle class is brand conscious and they shop with particular well-known brands in mind. In these middle class communities you will find your traditional brands like Chili's, Target, Petco and Best Buy just to name a few. These particular type of brands understand that the Middle Class spends more of their money with popular brands that they feel are tried and proven. Most Middle Class Citizens will choose not to shop with a start-up Tax Preparation Company because they take pride is letting their peers know that they either use a CPA to prepare their taxes or they go with a big brand like HR Block. I'm not suggesting that you can't be successful in a Middle Class community, but it may become a little harder to see success fast in these types of communities.

Lower To Moderate Economic Community

Based on my observations the most profitable tax locations are located in the lower to moderate economic area. It may be hard to believe, but the tax offices that are located in these low to moderate economic areas make the most profit, have the most customers and charge the highest fees.

The reason for this odd occurrence is based on a government tax credit called the **Earned Income Credit (EITC)** that was discussed earlier in this book. However, in short, the EITC gives a large refundable tax credit to an individual whose earnings are close to the poverty line in the form of refundable credit that allows low to moderate income customers to receive large tax returns to offset their wages.
In some cases a single person with three children who makes only $15,000 per year can receive a Tax Refund Check of approximately $8000 while having zero Federal Income dollars withheld from their paychecks.

Since EITC will more than likely occur in lower to moderate economic communities, Tax Business are taking advantage of this and setting up tax offices in these communities to share in the profits that these types of customers offer.

Thus I will always suggest that you start your Tax Preparation Business in a Lower to Moderate Economic Area. Let me share with you a situation that happens every year in my business.

When a new customer comes in and after the Tax Preparation service is completed, I always try to get feedback from my customers on why they chose to patronize my business this year. I usually experience the same two answers all the time. First they inform me that my business was easy to find and second, that they say they had their W2's in their back pocket looking for a company that they could file their tax return immediately and provide them with the best service needed to prepare their taxes.

How Can You Determine If You Are In a Lower to Moderate Economic Community That Best Supports A Tax Office?

Through my years of experience, I been able to determine what to look for to set up a profitable tax business in a lower to moderate economic community. If you see the following types of business in a certain community, more than likely you will be able to set up a profitable tax business:

- *Dollar Stores*
- *Fast-Food Restaurants*
- *Pawn Shops*

- *Video Stores*
- *Liquor Stores*
- *Walmart*
- *Rent-to-Own Business*
- *Check Cashing Companies*
- *Bargain Stores*

How Much Space Will You Need To Operate A Tax Business?

Don't get confused into believing that you need a large space in order to operate a tax business. I've seen successful tax location make Hundreds of Thousands of dollars in a 200 square foot unit with just enough room for two tax preparation desk and 4 customer chairs. Spaces like these are what we as Tax Preparation Business owners call **Gems**. We call them Gems based upon the small amount of rent we pay operate this location which always equal more profit.
When selecting a location please choose the smallest area that will adequately help you service your customers. The ideal size would be in a range of 700-1000 square feet.

What sets up most tax business to fail in business is the high amount of rent they must pay at a particular location. Remember, Tax Season is only four months, January through April. However you will more than likely be obligated to pay rent for that location the entire year. This is why I will always suggest you to find the best space for the lowest price.

The best price is usually tied to the smaller location.

Chapter 6

WHAT DOES THE PERFECT TAX CUSTOMER LOOK LIKE

If I told you that the Perfect Tax Customer usually makes between 8,000 dollars and 15,000 dollars per year would you believe me? Suppose I further informed you that the perfect tax customers will usually be unmarried and have between two and three children. Believe it or not, I've just given you the basis of what the Perfect Tax Customer looks like.

This Perfect Tax Customer will not be part of a particular race, have a specific gender or live in a certain region in the United States. In fact, the Perfect Tax Customer will include every race in the United States, to include Whites, Blacks Browns and Yellow. They will also live in every geographical location all across the country. Even though they may be different in various aspects, they will have one thing in common and that one thing is that they are living either close to, or under the poverty line. In other words, they are the working poor.

The working poor are the people who are employed, but they don't make enough take care of them and their families properly. Because they don't make enough, the US government has decided to assist them by giving them a refundable Tax Credit called the Earned Income Tax Credit.

In a nutshell, the Earned Income Credit is money in the form of a Tax Refund given to certain people who qualify. These Tax Refunds can range as high as $8,000 per tax return.

Example: A person with three children making $15,000 per year, paying about $1,000 in Federal Income Taxes may qualify for a Tax Refund between $8,000 and $9,999.

The Perfect Tax Customer needs one thing and they need their Refund money fast. This type of customer will need their money fast because during the year they may have found themselves behind in paying their rent, their children may need clothes, food or just simple relief.

Ask yourself this one question. If you were a customer that only made $15,000 per year with children and you knew you were entitled to a large refund check in the range of $8,000 - $9,999, would you really care about how much you paid a Tax Preparation Company to get your tax refund? Just think about it, The Perfect Tax Customer will expect to receive a Tax Refund check that may be equivalent to 50% of their total yearly income. That's the reason that they come in.

Also, suppose I told you that this type of Tax Return for this type of customer is one of the easiest to prepare. Most Tax Preparers can complete these type of tax returns within 15 minutes and charge and average price ranging from $350 – $700 per tax Return.

This alone is the reason why you see so many Tax Preparation Companies in these Lower to Moderate economic areas. In most of these poor areas, you will find, an Auto Parts Store, a 99 cent store, a Liquor Store and a Tax Preparation Business. Most of these Tax Preparation companies are concentrated in a particular area, because they know there's tremendous business to be had. Also these Tax Businesses have a better chance at success if they are located in the proximity of a good HR Block office, because Block has done all of the research for them and they know exactly where the Perfect Tax Customers resides.

The beauty of it is that your Tax Preparation Business can take a part of this as well. Studies have shown that The Perfect Tax Customer is not loyal to brands. The Perfect Tax Customer only needs to believe that you can get them the refund they deserve and you can get them that refund fast.

Thus every Tax Business can compete especially if you are a small company that can react to change quickly.

Just think about it. If you complete 100 tax returns at $350 per return you've made $35,000. If you complete 300 tax returns at $350, you've made $105,000. 300 tax returns can be completed by one Tax Preparer in a tax season. So if you are just getting started and you follow the plan you should be able to make $100,000 in the first 2 months of the year with only one Tax Preparer.

Chapter 7

SETTING UP YOUR TAX OFFICE

Exterior Set-Up

Setting up the exterior of your office is a must. It's the first impression that new clients will see, and will also help them determine how professional your tax preparation business is operated. It can also be used to drive customers into your business.

Signage

The proper [ss]. This is important [ ] help customers make sure [ace].

> **JOHN'S TAX SERVICE**
> **(213) 555-5555**

The signage I prefer and suggest that you use as well is the Lighted Box Sign. A Lighted Box sign is a sign that is placed on the outside your business or the facade of the individual unit you possess. It's lighted and it's easy to see from a distance. The Lighted Box Sign is a marketing tool that lets potential customers know exactly where your office is located during the daytime hours as well as the night.

There are two things that must be on your Lighted Box Sign. First, the sign must have the name of your Tax Business and second, it must have your Phone Number.

Example

Also make sure that when you choose the name of your Tax Business, that you place the word "Tax" or "Tax Service" in the name. This will help when potential customers are searching for the specific service you provide on the internet or other marketing outlets.

Don't give your Tax Business an abstract name that a normal person wouldn't be able to determine the actual service your business provides.

Also make sure to, place the telephone number on the entry door of your business along with your operation hours.

Interior Set-Up
The way the interior of your office is set up has just as much to do with the marketing of your business as the exterior.
Reception Desk

First, depending on the size of your office, you'll need a Reception Desk. The Reception desk should be the first desk that meet your client when they walk into your office. However, just because you have a reception desk, doesn't necessary mean that you need to hire a Receptionist? The Reception Desk acts as a barrier between the client walking into the Tax Office and the Tax Preparation Desk. The Reception Desk acts as a greeting point for all of your clients who may enter your business.

The reception desk will usually have items displayed on it like the Sign in-Sheets, pencils and pens and will act as a good starting point before you take your client to the Tax Preparation Desk. The Reception Desk also acts as an area for which clients can pick up items like their Tax Returns or their Tax Refund Checks.

Waiting Area

Chairs

You will need a minimum of 2-10 waiting room chairs. These chairs are placed in the front of the office away from the Tax Preparation area.

TV VCR Combination

You will need a small TV in your waiting area. Your television should constantly be on from the time you open until closing. The TV should be tuned into neutral channel like the News. The purpose of the TV is to keep your clients entertained while they are waiting to be served. The TV should be tuned to a station that won't offend any of your customers, especially children. I usually tune the TV to a station that plays the news constantly. You must understand that although you as the owner may enjoys sporting programs or an occasional cooking show, not all of your customers will feel entertained by your selection.

Also make sure that you keep a couple of G-Rated movies for the children that may come into your office. I've found out that if you keep the children of your clients entertained, it' make preparing their parents taxes extremely easy.

Children's Area

I like to set up a specific area in my office dedicated to the children who come in with their parents. In this area I will usually place a children table along with a couple of children chairs. The children's area will include Crayons, Coloring Books and other small toys to keep the children entertained.

Small Refrigerator

Tax clients like free stuff whether it be Logo T-Shirts, Logo Pens or anything free. To start the ball rolling I enjoy and encourage giving free stuff away to every customer that enter your office. Items may include free soda pop, water, coffee and snacks. I keep the refrigerator stocked at all times and offer my clients as much as they want. The price of a soda pop is about 25 cents per can if you purchase them in bulk at Costco's or Sam's Club.

Marketing Posters
I always decorate my office with marketing posters with people who look like they are having fun or materials that market my tax business.

NO Time Clocks
I never place a time clock in my Tax Preparation Business, due to the fact that if there's lots of customers that are waiting to be served, I don't want them to refer to the time clock to remind them how long they've been waiting for service.

Chapter 8

Dealing With Your Customer and Their Tax Return Money

If you are fortunate and able to locate your Tax Preparation Business in a lower to moderate economic community, congratulations, you're well on your way to great success. However, there are important things that you must be aware of when dealing with Tax Preparation Client that live in a lower to moderate economic area.

First, a lower to moderate income tax client will always need to be aware of every single step of the process regarding their tax refund. These particular customers may not possess all of the resources to look things up for themselves, so you as the Tax Preparation business must set up procedures in your office that facilitate effective communication between your office and your customers.

The Tax Preparation Client in the lower to moderate economic area may lack several things in comparison to your customers you come from a higher economic community. These differences may include Banks Accounts, Credit Cards and others specifics. You'll find out that most of your customers in these lower to moderate communities either cash their payroll checks at a Check Cashing facility or the local Walmart. Since the lower to moderate income client will more than likely lack certain resources, they will expect their tax refund check to be delivered to your office once it's ready to print.

The following are some of the procedures I follow when dealing with Lower to Moderate Income Clients.

Keeping Client Informed

You must keep your lower to moderate economic clients informed from the beginning of the tax preparation process until they come in and pick up their tax refund check.

IRS Accepted Tax Returns

Your first communication after the client's leaves your office will occur after you e-file the client's tax return and the IRS accepts it. Once your clients Tax Return is accepted by the IRS, it's simply means that the IRS has received the Tax Return on behalf of your client and there doesn't appear to be any problem with the tax return like someone using the clients Social Security Numbers on that tax return.

An IRS acceptance doesn't mean that the client will receive a refund, it only means they accept the tax return on its face and will try to process the Tax Return.

Never Make Refund Promises to Your Customers

The IRS states that most Tax Returns should be processed and a refund should be issued within 20 days. Let me emphasize this statement one more time. The IRS states that **most** tax returns and refunds will be processed within 20 days, not all.

This is extremely important and it comes into play when you process a customer's tax return and your Tax Preparer states to the client that they will have their refund in 20 days.

This is when it may become dangerous for your Tax Business. **You cannot make a promise to a client to ensure what the IRS will or will not do. You don't control the IRS.** If you promise something to someone and you can't control the outcome, more than likely at some point you may find yourself in trouble especially if the client relies on your promise and that promise never happens. You may find yourself faced with a very angry client.

The Tax Client who relied on your promise to receive a tax refund within 20 days may have made other promises to others relying on your promise to them. The Tax Client may have promised to pay their landlord back rent, pay a late payment for a car note or even a loan payment to someone.

You can never make a guarantee to any client that they will either receive a refund on that they will receive a refund by a certain date. You can't guarantee that a client will receive a tax Refund at all. It's all up to the IRS.

Never Hold On To Client Checks

Your low to moderate income client will more than likely need their tax refund before they receive it. Therefore certain procedures must be established to ensure that they receive their tax refund as soon as you are authorized to give it to them. I'm talking minutes not hours.

As soon as you are authorized to give a client a check you must do it immediately. This act alone will build a good relationship with you and your clients and they will more than likely return year after year because of your good business practices.

I've experienced customers coming into my tax office requesting their income tax check literally one minute after I called the customer and notified them that their check was ready for pick-up. I've also observed customers coming in angrily asking for their tax refund check that they knew you had in your possession and never informed them that you had it.

Calling Customers

A calling customer procedure must be in place before you open your office. The following are the specific times that you should call your customers:
- Acceptance of Their Tax Return By the IRS
- Rejection of The Tax Return By The IRS
- Acceptance of Their Tax Return By the State
- Rejection of The Tax Return By The State
- Clients IRS Check Is Ready For Pick up
- Client State Check Is Ready For Pick Up
- Client IRS Check is Scheduled For Direct Deposit
- Client State Check Is Scheduled For Direct Deposit

There are other time when you may have to call a client, but if you make these basic calls, you will definitely be on your way to a good Tax Season.

Chapter 9

Choosing Your Phone Service
(Controlling Your Cost)

When I first opened my Tax Business, I found out that there were many business trying to make money from me, and I had yet to even open for business.

I was solicited by Credit Card Processing Companies, Payroll Services, Web Site Builders and many other type of businesses. If I had chosen to patronize all of the companies that wanted me to do business with them, I would be in debt and broke before I evened opened. However there was one critical service that I knew I needed and that one important item was great phone service.

Operating a business phone line can be quite expensive if you don't know how to maneuver correctly. It's true that in order for your business to survive, you will need a phone number. When I first opened my business, my telephone bill was about $100 per month for basic business phone service and I had no other choice to pay that amount every month if I wanted to stay in business. If I failed to pay bill, my phone line would become disconnected and my customers couldn't contact me.

I found two problems with this scenario. First the price of business phone service was too expensive and if I had to move my business to a new location, it was hard for to keep the same telephone number possibly resulting in the loss of a great deal of clients.

I looked into securing a different type of phone service that was cheaper and that would meet all of my needs. I looks and found out about Voice over Internet Phone Service (VOIP). With this type of phone service, all I needed was an active Internet Provider. The VOIP service had everything I needed and more for a fraction of the price. I decided to go with the Vonage Home Plan, **not the Vonage Business Plan**, because the home plan was less expensive.

The Vonage Home Plan provided me with following features:
- A Phone Number That I Could Take Anywhere
- A Smaller Monthly Fee
- Ability to Block Calls
- Ability to Forward Call To My Cell Phone during Off Hours
- Ability To Check Voice Mails Remotely

Now during the off season if a client needed their taxes prepared and they called my office number, I was able to answer the call because all of the calls were forwarded to my cell phone. I found out that this alone assisted me in securing a great deal of extra business because know I was able to answer the call even though I wasn't in the office.
I also secured lots of new customers using this method, because it's hard to get in contact with most Tax Preparation office during the off Season. Customer have informed me, that before they finally reached my tax business, they tried all of the major Tax Preparation Companies and no one answered or returned their calls.

As a small business owner, you'll need the ability to be flexible and service customers that your competitors will neglect. Just by adding this particular type of phone service has guaranteed me that I will serve new customers constantly all year round. It's also given my business the opportunity to secure more revenue through tax preparation fees.

Chapter 10
The Tax Preparation Period
(Tax Season)

Tax Season is a big deal. This is the time of the year when the economy take a huge up swing. If you ever get a chance to sit back and observe the start of Tax Season, you will notice that the majority of businesses start to advertise and try to direct traffic to their business during this time period.

Have you ever observed the behavior of businesses like Furniture Companies, Car Lots, Clothing Stores, Mattress Centers, Restaurants and other business during Tax Season?

Most of these businesses embark on a heavy ad campaign around this time. It's like these business know that money is on its way and they are waiting for the money to circulate into their business. In fact, most business rely on Tax Season for a significant part of their annual revenues.

It's extremely important that you as a Tax Business know when Tax Season begins and ends to include all Peak and Non Peak periods.

The Tax business is one of the most predictable businesses in the country. It so predictable, you can set you clock to it. In fact, in this chapter, I will inform you the time periods and the days you'll receive the majority of your customers and the days for which you will see the least amount of customers. Tax season begins on January 15th through April 15th each year. However it's subject to change by the IRS occasionally.

There are two times for which I know that the IRS Tax season may be delayed, the beginning of Tax Season and the end of Tax Season.

On some occasions the IRS has taken the liberty of changing the e-file start date. This start date may change when there is a significant change in a Federal Law that affect taxes. This delay usually occurs if the IRS feels they don't have enough time to update their systems to handle the new changes.

Also the IRS may change the ending date to file a Tax return beyond the April 15th deadline. There are two common reasons why the ending date to file a tax return may change.

First, if April 15th happens to fall on a Saturday or Sunday, the last day to file a tax return is extended to the end of the next business day. For example, if April 15th fall on a Saturday, the tax filing deadline is extended until 11:59 pm, Monday April 17th.

There is another reason for an extended filing date and it's based on a Federal Holiday that is observed in Washington DC called Emancipation Day.
"Emancipation Day is a holiday in Washington DC to mark the anniversary of the signing of the Compensated Emancipation Act which President Abraham Lincoln signed on April 16th, 1982. It is annually held on April 16th."

For Example if April 15th fall on a Saturday, Emancipation day falls on Sunday, the Observance for Emancipation day will fall on the next business day which will be Monday, April 17th. Thus Tax Season will be extended until 11:59 pm, Tuesday April 18th.

As I stated earlier Tax Season is very predictable once it's get started. I will break down the calendar of Tax Season in 4 different categories, Regular Tax Season, 1st Peak, 2nd Regular Tax Season and 2nd Peak.

1st Regular Tax Season - January 15th – January 25th
1st Peak - January 25th – February 15th.
2nd Regular Tax Season - February, 16th – April 6th.
2nd Peak - April 7th – April 15th or the last day of Tax Season.

1st Regular Tax Season - January 15th – January 25th

This is the time when the IRS begins to accept Electronic Filings. Most people at this time will not have their W2's and won't be ready to file their Tax Return at this time. However, some people may have their W2's and all of the documents

needed and are ready and willing to file. During this time you will
conduct about 10% of your business as a Tax Preparation Company.

1st Peak - January 25th – February 15th.

The 1st Peak will be your busiest period and it will last for approximately 2 - 3 weeks. At this time most people will start receiving their W2's forms and are trying to file their tax returns immediately. The type of customers that you'll see at this time will appreciate fast service and more than likely are expecting a refund. They will more than likely expect their refund fast and in a hurry. This is the time when most Tax Preparers work long hours and service the majority of their customers. During this time, your Tax Business will be conducting about 60% of your business.

So between the start of Tax Season up until February 15th, most tax business have conducted 70% of their business.

2nd Regular Tax Season - February, 16th – April 6th

During the 2nd Regular Tax Period you will find a slowdown in clients coming into your business. Now you will experience a different kind of customer. These customers will appear to be more established. They will probably own their homes, have higher paying jobs and their tax return will be more complexed. The customer that enters your business on the 2nd Regular Tax Season differs from your 1st Peak tax client in that the 2nd Regular Tax Season customer is not interested in speed or the desire for their tax refund to come back fast. These customers are more concerned with the Tax Preparers accuracy and professionalism.

These customer will more than likely bring in all of their tax documents and expect you to find as many legal tax deductions they may qualify for. This is when a Tax Preparer must become even more professional and able to communicate their abilities to the customer. Your business will experience about 20% of its business during this period.

2nd Peak - April 7th – April 15th or the last day of Tax Season

The last part of your Tax Season you will experience all of your procrastinator or the people who know they will owe the IRS money. You will get a mixture of all type of clients at this time. You will service clients that want their refund fast and clients who want their Tax Return to be prepared accurately.

You'll get busier and busier as the filing deadline approaches so get your staff ready for the busy days ahead. You'll conduct 10% of your business during this one week.

I also wanted to reiterate that Tax Season is unlike any other business because you only see your customers once a year. If you fail to prepare and take advantage of 1st Peak you will miss 60% of your business and thus have a poor Tax Season so make sure that you're prepared

Chapter 11

Marketing Your Tax Business

It will be extremely difficult for your Tax Preparation Business to become successful without being extremely focused on getting the word out about your business. I suggest that you place marketing of your business at the top of the list.

If your Tax Preparation Business doesn't start attracting customers immediately, you'll soon be out of business. So to make sure that your business becomes successful out of the gate, I will share with you seven (7) areas that will ensure that your business becomes successful.

1. Hire a Professional Tax Preparer

A Professional Tax Preparer is more than a person that knows how to prepare taxes. You'll probably find out that you can teach almost anyone how to prepare taxes with the new step by step modern tax software, however, you can't teach someone to be a Professional Tax Preparer if they don't have a clue as to what a Professional Tax Preparer looks like.

When a client comes in to your Tax Business and need your service, they are trusting you with a great deal of sensitive information. The client is trusting you with their Social Security Number not only for them but their spouse and their children. They are trusting you with their W2 forms which states how much they make and where they work. They're trusting you with their address and all type of personal and sensitive information, so just knowing how to prepare taxes isn't enough.

Studies have shown that customers come back year after year not because of the Tax Preparation Company, but for the Tax Preparer that prepares their taxes each and every year. It's the bond that the Tax Preparer has with the client. This is true so much so, that customers are known to follow their Tax Preparers to different companies based on the close relationship between the Tax Preparer and their Clients.

When a client walks into your establishment and needs their taxes prepared, they are looking for two things. The first thing they will analyze will occur just by looking at you. During this first client analyses, they will determine whether you have the capability to prepare their taxes to their specification.

The second thing the Tax Client will analyze is your trust worthiness. They will determine if you look like a person of good character and someone they can trust. If a Tax Preparer meets these two requirement at the initial meet, the client will usually allow you the Tax Preparer to prepare their taxes.

So let me show you how it works. At the initial contact the Tax Preparer must look professional. That means, they must were slacks or a skirt, a blouse or a dress shirt with dress shoes. Make sure that the Tax Preparer has a nice pair of shoes and is groomed well. A Tax Preparer should never were jeans, athletic shoes or shorts when dealing with clients.

The second thing that they must overcome is the knowledge aspect of the initial meeting. A Tax Preparer must display confidence in their profession. This means they must convey to the client that they know exactly what they are doing and can handle any type of tax problem better than anyone else. The client must also be able to trust you with their sensitive information before they start. This is conveyed to the client by your professionalism.

2. Business to Business Marketing (B2B)

Our next marketing plan used to attract customers is our B2B which builds relationships with neighboring businesses.

The main reason we use B2B is to create a reciprocal relationship between our Tax Preparation Business and the other businesses in the area. By conducting B2B, you will not only let other businesses in your community know where you're located, but also let them know what you are doing and how you can help them.

When conducting B2B there are several steps that must be followed to make this an effective form of marketing that works for your Tax Business.

- Ask what your Tax Preparation Company can do for the other business first.
- Collect marketing items from their business and give them to your customers.
- Build a rapport with the business.
- Try to get to know the people in the business.
- Try to establish a connection between you and the business.
- Remember, that no one cares about you, until you show that you care about them.

3. Person to Person (P2P)

P2P works similar to B2B but you are actually approaching potential customers on the street. You can ask them question like:
1. "Have your taxes been prepared yet?"
2. "Have they heard of your business?"
3. Do you know the location of your tax preparation Business?"

Point to the direction of your business and inform them of any specials your tax business is currently running. You will want to give each person you come into contact with a coupon or a business card at this time.

4. Seminars

The purpose of a seminar is to position yourself and your tax office as the experts in your community. It is also used as a method of giving back to the community.

You can conduct a seminar on various topics to include the tax related issues of a Day Care Facility, a Barbershop, and Realtors to name a few. These seminars can be conducted almost anywhere. If you do it correctly, you will build better community relationships, establish expertise, see your revenue increase and become a better presenter.

5. A Sign Waver (Marketer)

A sign waver is a human marketer that stand in front of your business waving a sign with advertises your business. This is a proven method that is guaranteed to draw client into your business.

This is how it works. You will hire a person by the hour to stand on the sidewalk waving a sign to all passersby's informing them that you are in business and the sign will communicate what you actually do.
The person you hire to hold the sign may say the following:

- Fast Tax Preparation
- Accurate Tax Preparation
- No Waiting
- Get Money Fast

Please be creative with the signs and make sure it looks as professional as possible. Don't create handwritten sign because that will make your business look unprofessional. The Sign waver should be place in front of your business during high traffic times and they should be consistently out in front of the business.

I've heard that it can take a possible client 9 times to see your advertisement before they notice who you are and what you're selling. However, when they do see it, they will know where to go if they need your service.

6. Exterior Visibility

Not only will you want a box sign affixed to your location, you will also want to enhance the visibility of your location by adding marketing items out and around your location. The following are ways you can make your location more visible to attract more customers:

- Wind Feathers with the word Tax Preparation on them
- Any Lighted Sign Places outside of your office
- American Flags
- Pennants attached you Your Business
- Marketing balloon on Top of Your Business.

If you ever seen a good Car Lot and notice how they enhance the outside of their business, will give you the best example on how to market your business.

7. Interior Decorum

There no simple way to put it. Your Interior Decorum must be clean and modern. Don't invest in old used furniture or desk. I'm not saying that your furniture has to be expensive, but it must be modern. You can find good looking modern office furniture at stores like IKEA. The furniture may not be of the best quality but it will give your office that clean and modern office feel.

Chapter 12

The Attributes of the Effective Tax Preparer

The Tax Preparer is the essential element in order to have an effective Tax preparation Company. If you hire the wrong Tax Preparer, it's hard to operate a lucrative Tax Preparation Business. There are 4 ingredients that all Tax Preparers must possess. If you're Tax Preparer doesn't possess these attributes, it's hard to get to the bread and butter and create a year after year successful tax business, which is based upon Customer Retention. The 4 elements of an effective Tax Preparer are the <u>Tax Preparer Appearance</u>, the <u>Tax Preparer Knowledge</u>, the <u>Tax Preparer Communication</u> and the ability for the <u>Tax Professional to be Personal</u>.

Tax Preparer Appearance

Appearance is the outward impression that you convey to someone. In the Tax Business, first impressions are key. When a client enters your establishment, they are looking for help. The client is trying to determine whether you have the appropriate skills set to fix their problem, and the first thing they will observe is your appearance.

A Tax Preparer does not have to put on a suit and tie, but they should look professional. I recommend that all tax preparers were dress slack or a skirt and a collard shit or a blouse. At no time should a tax preparer were jeans, athletic gym suits or T-shirts. I also suggest that you invest in a uniformed logo shirt representing your tax business which will better represent your business and give you that look of professionalism.

Tax Preparer Knowledge

A Tax Preparer must possess the expert knowledge on how to prepare taxes. If this modern world of Tax Preparation, you don't have to be great with tax calculations like tax preparers had to be about 20 years ago. Back then taxes were prepared with pencil and paper and were mailed to the IRS. Nowadays everything is done on computers and the computer calculates everything for you. Also you don't necessary have to mail your tax return to the IRS, you can e-file your tax returns and the IRS will receive the tax returns instantly.

The Tax Computer programs are so easy to operate, that a novice can be an expert in no time. Preparing taxes on Computer Software is just like learning a new computer program.

When I first open my first tax office, I never prepared a tax return in my life. I attended training on how to operate a tax business, but little did I know that the training would never teach me how to prepare taxes. When I asked the instructor on the last day of training, "When would we learn how to prepare taxes," he responded, "There's no need to teach you how to prepare taxes, because the computer program does the tax preparation for you."

So I started thinking, if the Computer program did the Tax Return for my clients, then what would I have to do? At that time I found out that the modern Tax Preparer is really a Data Entry person with knowledge of how to manipulate the tax computer program.

Just imagine a client who enters your office and needs their taxes prepared. This Tax Client is a low income client with three children and only makes about $15,000 per year. If you prepare their taxes correctly, they may receive a Tax Refund of $8,000 or higher. When they receive their refund, they'll use the money to catch up on bills and to help their children. Since this particular client needs this money to survive and take care of their family, they will not entrust certain tax preparers with the task of preparing their taxes if the tax preparer can't communicate to the client and give the client the result they're looking for. If the client feels that you lack the necessary knowledge to help them, they will simply walk out of your business and look for someone else who can get the job done.

The knowledge aspect come in as you communicate to the client that you understand what documents they have, what needs to be filed, and what you estimate their Tax Return to be. This conveys to the tax client that you as the Tax

Preparers know exactly what's going on and you can help them reach their tax preparation goals.

Tax Preparer Communication

Communication means the ability to take part of. Most people who desire to prepare taxes as a professional don't think that this element is needed in preparing taxes, however thinking like this is completely wrong.

In the old days people looked at Tax Preparers as people that were exceptional in math and lack the ability to communicate effectively, somewhat like a Nerd. This may have been true in the past and I still see some people like this in some of the chained franchised tax preparing companies. You've seen the type, they may be wearing slacks with a short sleeved shirt and a pencil protector in the shirt pocket. These types of Tax Preparers don't have a desire to communicate with the customer and in some cases they believe that they are doing you a favor. They don't allow you to asked question and they believe they know what's best for you without even asking you for your opinion. In most cases the client is scared to ask this type of Tax Preparer any questions and thus a bad relationship is formed.

However, in modern times, the Tax Preparer who doesn't have the ability to communicate with their clients can't be effective.

The modern Tax Preparer must be able to hold a conversation with all of their clients. They must be approachable and display the desire to listen. They must be able to analyze their client needs and be able to express to their clients they understand their needs. This new type of communication is best describe as active listening. I instruct all of my Tax Preparers to spend the first five minutes of the Tax Preparation Session listening to their client needs and only after that period shall they communicate to the client what they can and will do to assist them.

A Tax Preparer must be a Personal Person

A personal person is a person that is able to relate to other people easily. A tax client wants to be able to like the person who is preparing their taxes. After all they are entrusting you with a great deal of personal information, like Social Security Numbers and other private information.

One way you can be personal with your client is by trying to find things that you have in common with them. I usually start out talking about the weather, if it's cold, hot, snowing or raining.

If it's a client who likes sports, I will start off by talking about the local sport team. If I find it difficult to hold a conversation naturally with the client, I will always ask them about their family. I found out that by discussing the client family, like their children and their children's successes, will always spark a great conversation and build rapport.

Customer Retention

Finally, if you hire a Tax Preparer that possesses all of the above qualities, you will get what every business owner wants and must have to be successful year after year, and that's Customer Retention.

Customer Retention means holding on to a customer year after year. Regarding marketing, the cheapest cost to get a customer to walk in your door is the returning customer.

The Tax Business is unique. It's not like owing a grocery store or a gas station were the customers come back every week. The Tax Business is different because, a tax client only has to file a Tax Return once a year. This means that you only get one shot to get that customer in your office. So as a Tax Preparation Business owner, you will always desire to secure the customer who came to you the previous year and want them to come again each and every year. This is the beauty of customer retention. If you have a Tax Preparer who possess all of the positive the traits stated earlier, you have a higher probability of retaining that customer year after year.

Chapter 13

Don' Be Afraid To Charge a Profitable Fee!

I use to believe that the less you charge for Tax Preparation, the more customers you would service thus, the more money you would receive. If you believe in the basic principles on how a business should work, you will more than likely share the same belief that I had long ago.

The first year I opened my Tax Preparation business, I serviced 400 client. I grossed $60,000 as was quite happy until it was time to pay all of my bills and keep my business opened. When I calculated the average fee I charged for a single Tax Return, it came out to be approximately $150. I'm ashamed to say that I thought a $150 fee for a Tax Return was too high. I also remember it being hard for me to ask my clients to pay $150 for my service.

My mistaken belief was that if I charged $150 per tax return, I would retain a high percentage of customers for the next Tax Season and thus build my business year after year. Man was I wrong!

When the next year rolled around, I only retained about 25% of my prior year customers. Most of my customers that didn't return chose to patronize higher priced Tax Preparation companies. I was puzzled. I asked myself, "Why a customer would chose to pay twice as much for a Tax Return and receive the exact same Refund that I would give them if they patronized my business?"

I set out to get feedback from my customers to find out the reason they chose not to come back to my company the following year.

All of the prior year customers I surveyed believed that I had nice clean and professional office. I matched up with everything that the others companies had to offer besides one critical thing, and that one thing was that I lacked confidence in my product and services and I displayed that lack of confidence in my product and service by failing to present my fee confidently.

Due to my lack of confidence, my clients were led to believe that they were receiving an inferior product or Tax Return.

It was my customer's belief that since I didn't have the confidence to charge a fee similar to my competitors, there had to be something wrong with my service or my product, and they didn't want to take a chance with me the following year.

I learned a valuable lesson that year and I had to change quickly. Immediately, I changed my pricing and charged an equivalent or higher fee that the National Tax Companies charged like HR Block.

I found out that my client believed that the higher you charge for a Tax Return the better your product.

If HR Block or Jackson Hewitt were charging $300 for a tax return, I would charge a similar price.

There are two rules of thumb as it pertains to the pricing a Tax Return. The rule is:

- **If 10% of your customers complain about your pricing being too high, then you are priced just right.**

- **If less than 10% of your customers complain about your pricing, you aren't charging enough.**

Pricing your service is critical for success.

Things That Occur When You Fail To Price Correctly

Most Independent Tax business go out of business not because of their service or they lack customers. Independent tax business fail because they don't have enough money to operate properly year after year.

I heard most people say that a new business is not supposed to be profitable in its first 3 years of existence. I beg to differ. I believe that if you're not profitable immediately, you'll go out of business.

As a Tax Preparation Business you'll have a great amount of expenses. The highest expenses will usually be your rent and paying your employees. We all know that Tax Businesses are usually only open between the months of January through April, but the rent still has to be paid for the full year despite the fact that you may not be conducting business between May and December.

There is a reason why National Tax Chains can pay rent for the entire year although they're only open January through April. The reason the National Tax Preparation Chains survive year after year is because they charge a high enough tax preparation fee to pay all of the bill which may include rents, utilities, employee benefits and miscellanies expenses and still make a profit. You must operate your business the same way!

As a Tax Preparation Business you'll want to charge a high enough fee so by the end of the Tax Season, you'll have made enough money to pay your rent, utilities, employee benefits and more, while still taking home a nice hardy profit so you can operate year after year.

Made in the USA
San Bernardino, CA
15 July 2018